EWE

by R. W. Metlen

HiddenSpring

ISBN: 978-1-58768-054-0

Published by

HiddenSpring

An Imprint of Paulist Press
997 Macarthur Boulevard
Mahwah, New Jersey 07430

www.hiddenspring.com

Printed and bound in the United States of America

Psalm 23

For Heidi

Hey!

Yeah, Ewe.

Ewe's a sheep.

That's what Ewe is.

And, like most sheep,
Ewe's got a shepherd.

His name is David.

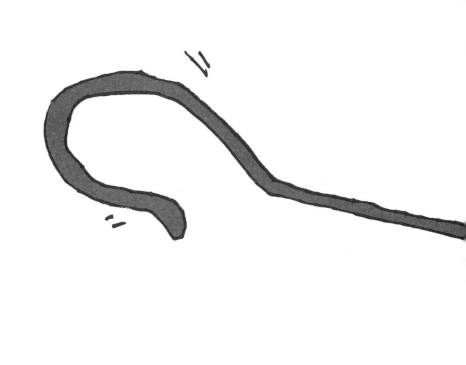

David is a good shepherd.

He loves Ewe no matter what.

No "ifs," "ands," or "maybes."

BZZZzzZ Shear
Shear
Shear

No "except whens" or "buts."

That's good, because
Ewe is not perfect!

e e c H !

Not even close.

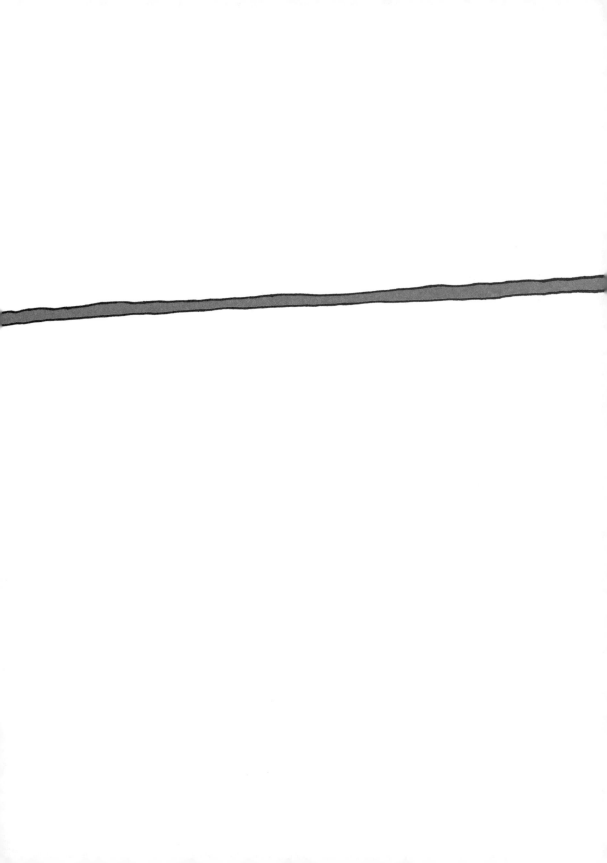

shuffle
shuffle

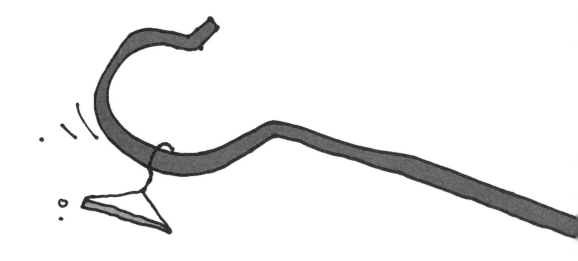

But David still loves Ewe...

...from Ewe's head
to Ewe's toes.

David would do anything to keep Ewe safe.

He'd fight lions,

or tigers,

or dragons,

or snakes!

Without David, these beasts would eat Ewe, of course.

Still, most of Ewe's problems come from a more dastardly source.

Take a look inside, Ewe...

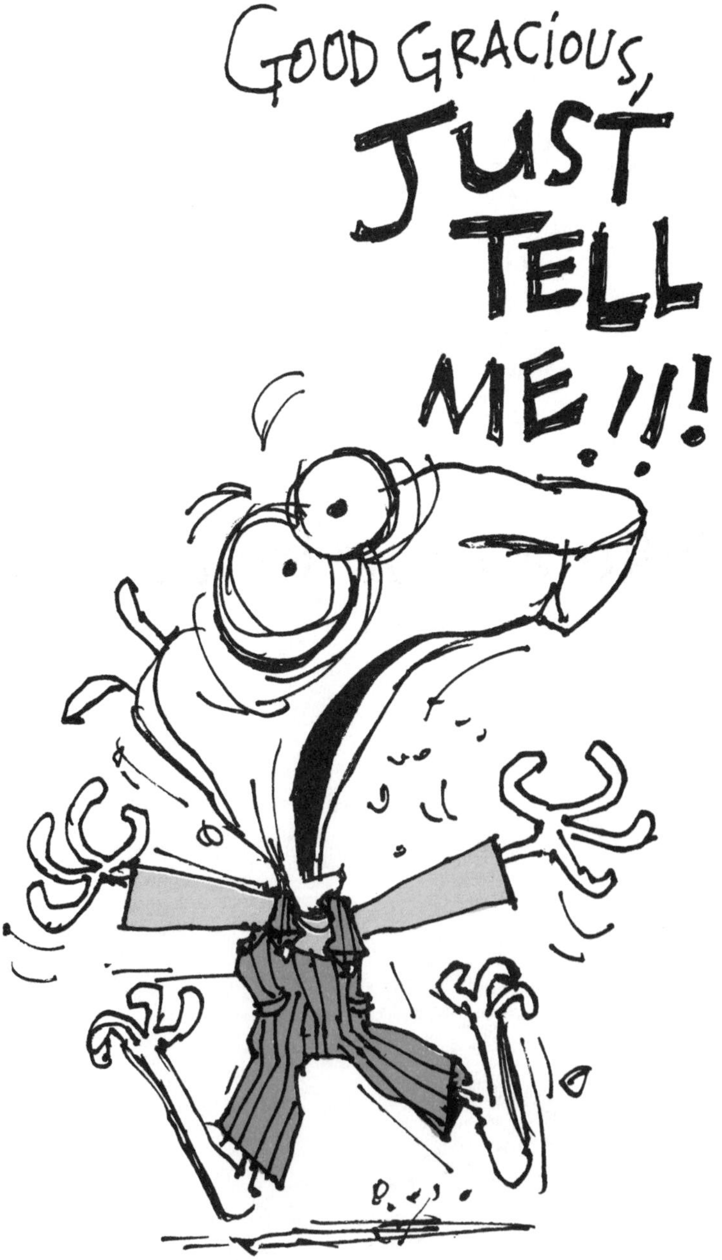
GOOD GRACIOUS,
JUST TELL ME!!!

...and Ewe'll surely see.

Ewe's own self is
Ewe's worst enemy!

Ewe seems skeptical.
Can't Ewe hear the truth?

Listen up, Ewe, because
here comes the proof.

When David says,
"Come here, Ewe,"
Ewe tends to stay.

If David says, "Stay there,
Ewe," Ewe wanders away...

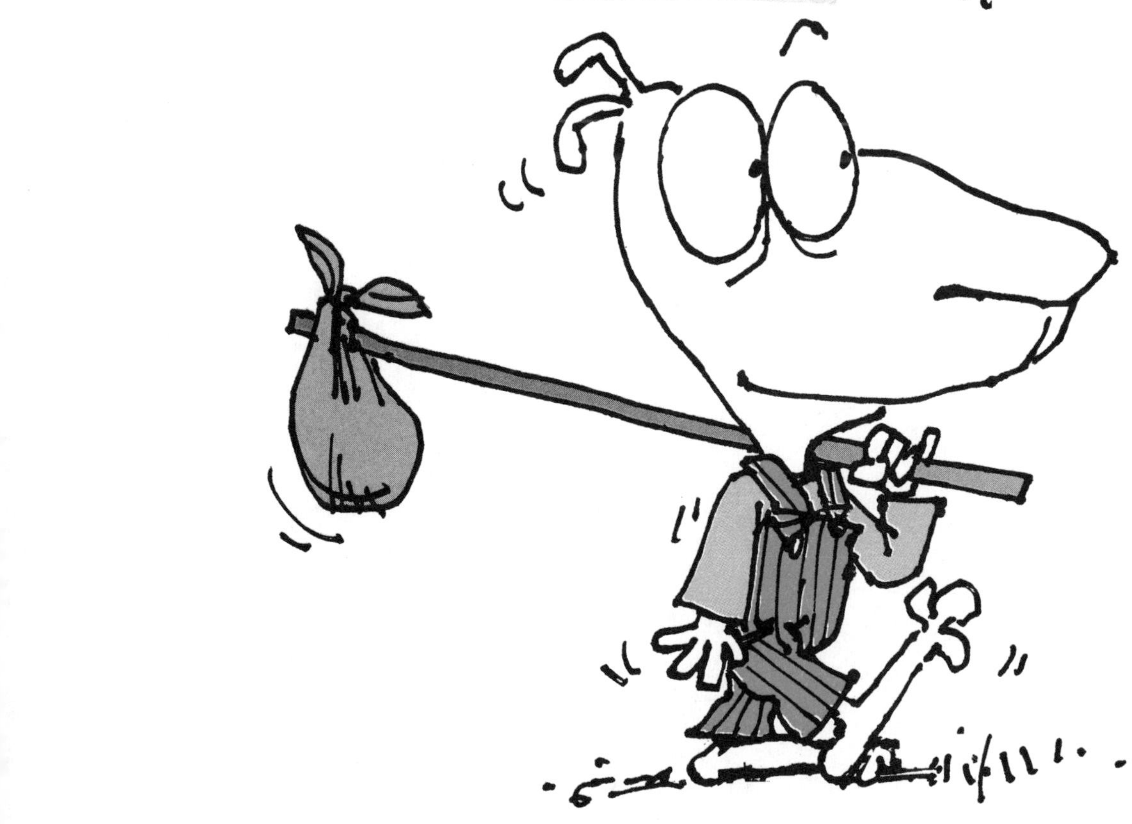

...and away...

...until Ewe is lost.

Uh-oh.

Ewe is in trouble.

HONK!
SCREECH!
WRONG WAY
click
click
click
HONK!
DO NOT ENTER
BEEP!
CAUTION
YIELD
BEEP
BEEP

Ewe
rethinks
some
of the
choices
Ewe's
made.

"David, where are you? Help me!" Ewe cries.

Without a moment to lose,
the good shepherd arrives!

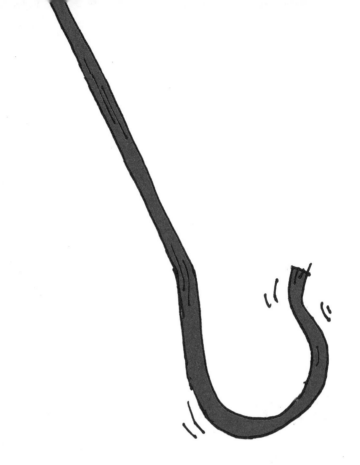

Ewe is rescued!

David saves the day!

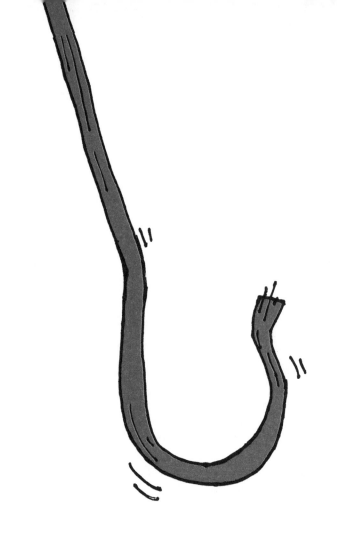

But now Ewe feels bad.

After all, Ewe did go astray.

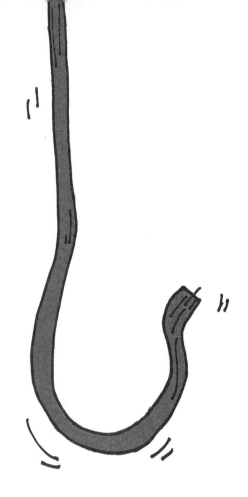

"David," Ewe says (how else but sheepishly), "I'm sorry for not listening. Will you ever forgive me?"

Then, like each time before
—without one exception ever—
David says, "Of course, I will.
I'm your shepherd, remember?"

And...

"No matter how far you go,
no matter where you go to,

no matter when it occurs,
or what you may do...

I will always and forever
love you, Ewe."

Ewe smiles because
Ewe knows it's true.

Ewe is a sheep.

That's what Ewe is.

Ewe's got a best friend.

Do you know his name?